RONALD REAGAN

ENCYCLOPEDIA
of PRESIDENTS

Ronald Reagan

Fortieth President of the United States

By Zachary Kent

Consultant: Charles Abele, Ph.D.
Social Studies Instructor
Chicago Public School System

CHILDRENS PRESS ®
CHICAGO

Reagan and wife Nancy watch election returns on November 4, 1980.

Library of Congress Cataloging-in-Publication Data

Kent, Zachary.
  Ronald Reagan / by Zachary Kent.
    p.   cm. — (Encyclopedia of presidents)
  Summary: A biography of the former motion picture actor who
served two terms as the fortieth president of the United States.
  ISBN 0-516-01373-4
  1. Reagan, Ronald—Juvenile literature.   2.   Presidents—
United States—Biography—Juvenile literature.   3.   United
States—Politics and government—1981-1989—Juvenile
literature.   [1.   Reagan, Ronald.   2.   Presidents.]
I. Title. II. Series.
E877.K46 1989
973.927'092—dc20   89-33746
[B]   CIP
[92]   AC

Picture Acknowledgments

AP/Wide World Photos, Inc.—4, 5, 6, 9, 11, 16,
28 (bottom), 31, 32, 35 (top), 37, 41 (2 photos),
44 (top), 45, 47 (2 photos), 57 (2 photos), 60, 63
(2 photos), 64, 65, 66, 67, 68, 70 (bottom), 74,
76, 80 (left), 81, 83, 86 (bottom), 88 (2 photos),
89 (top)

The Bettmann Archive—18, 24, 28 (top), 35
(bottom), 38

UPI/Bettmann Newsphotos—8, 13 (2 photos),
14, 19, 22, 44 (bottom), 49, 50, 55, 62, 70 (top),
71, 72, 73, 77, 79 (2 photos), 80 (right), 85, 86
(top), 89 (bottom)

U.S. Bureau of Printing and Engraving—2

Cover design and illustration
by Steven Gaston Dobson

Chief Justice Warren Burger administers the presidential oath
to Ronald Reagan on January 20, 1981.

Table of Contents

Chapter 1

"Six Shots Rang Out"

Outside the Hilton Hotel in Washington, D.C., on March 30, 1981, news reporters, cameramen, and photographers jostled for position. Curious bystanders also pressed close, hoping for the chance to glimpse President Ronald Reagan. In office only seventy days, Reagan was addressing a luncheon of labor union leaders that afternoon at a meeting inside the Hilton's International Ballroom.

At 2:30 P.M. the waiting crowd on the hotel sidewalk buzzed with rising excitement. Reporters quickly tested microphones, and parents lifted children for a better view. Soon Secret Service agents and White House aides stepped from a nearby doorway. Within seconds Reagan also walked out onto the sidewalk. Everyone easily recognized the president's warm smile and thick, dark hair. Reagan waved to the people, and cameras clicked as he crossed toward his limousine.

Suddenly, though, a crack of gunfire shattered the pleasant scene. A crazed assassin named John Hinckley, Jr. leaned through the crowd firing a .22-caliber pistol. "Six shots rang out," newswoman Sara Fritz remembered, "two quick ones followed by four in a steady rhythm. A puff of smoke rose in the air and people screamed, 'Get down, get back!' Bystanders . . . cowered against the hotel wall."

Opposite page: A Secret Service agent yells orders after shots were fired at Reagan.

Timothy McCarthy (left) and James Brady (front) lie wounded.

One bullet smashed into the head of White House press secretary James Brady. Another ripped into the neck of police officer Thomas Delahanty. Secret Service agent Timothy McCarthy spun around and tried to shield Reagan with his own body. A bullet tore into McCarthy's abdomen, and he also dropped to the sidewalk. Secret Service agent Jerry Parr instantly threw himself onto the startled president and shoved him through the open car door. The two men landed heavily on the backseat floor. "Take off!" shouted Parr to the driver. "Just take off!"

Secret Service agents scramble to get Reagan into the limousine.

As the limousine raced away, police and Secret Service men wrestled the gunman to the ground amid screaming and confusion. Inside the speeding car Reagan soon protested, "Jerry get off me. You're hurting my ribs. You really came down hard on top of me." Agent Parr helped the president into the rear seat. A few seconds later Reagan again complained of pain. "He was getting ashen color," remembered Parr. "Then he started to cough up some blood." Parr ordered the driver to rush to nearby George Washington University Hospital.

Reagan looked pale as he entered the hospital emergency room at 2:35 P.M. After walking several yards his knees buckled and he sagged to the floor. "I can't catch my breath," he gasped as anxious nurses and bodyguards lifted him onto a stretcher. Hurriedly emergency room staff cut away Reagan's clothes and searched for the cause of his injury. Dr. Wesley Price soon discovered a small jagged hole in Reagan's left side a few inches below his armpit. The president had been shot. Dr. Joseph Giordano swiftly inserted a tube into the wound to drain the blood filling Reagan's lung. Great quantities of bright red blood poured out of the president's chest. X-ray pictures soon revealed that, after striking one of Reagan's ribs, the bullet had passed into his lower left lung just inches from his heart.

By three o'clock, First Lady Nancy Reagan anxiously reached her husband's side. "Honey, I forgot to duck," he joked, hoping to ease her fears. Clearly, though, emergency surgery was needed to stop the bleeding and save the president's life. Hospital staff members made hurried preparations. Soon nurses wheeled Reagan's stretcher to Operating Room 2 and gently lifted him onto the table. As several doctors crowded close, Reagan joked again. "Please tell me you're all Republicans," he said, referring to his political party.

A lifetime of healthful exercise had left the seventy-year-old Reagan in fine physical condition. But since he had lost so much blood, the operation still would be dangerous. Dr. David Adelberg administered anesthesia, and the unconscious president was turned onto his right

Distraught, and bringing jelly beans, Nancy Reagan comes to visit her husband.

side. With a scalpel Dr. Ben Aaron sliced a six-inch cut across the left side of the patient's chest. Assistants inserted a stainless-steel rib spreader to stretch an opening between Reagan's ribs. After clearing out clotted blood, Dr. Aaron located the hole in the president's lung. Through many tense minutes the surgeon probed with his fingers, searching for the bullet. At last Dr. Aaron carefully drew out the flattened slug. Immediately the emergency team worked to close the wound, and after two tense hours the operation finally ended.

Later, although in pain and unable to speak, the president never lost his sense of humor. "Am I alive?" he teased in a scribbled note. The next morning nurses wheeled Reagan to a private room. "The President was a lot sicker than most people realized," said one doctor.

The news that other men had been wounded in the attack deeply saddened the kindhearted president. He knew, however, that the nation must keep moving forward. "The world has not stopped just because of this," he stated. The day after surgery he signed a congressional farm bill into law, and the next day he conducted a White House staff meeting at his bedside. Through the following week he performed many other chores from his hospital room. Doctors and nurses marveled as they watched the hardy old man regain his strength. On April 11, only twelve days after the shooting, relieved Americans learned of the president's release from the hospital.

Ronald Reagan's good humor and courageous spirit during his shocking ordeal greatly impressed citizens across the country. "He will be stronger politically because now he is a national hero on top of being President," guessed Congressman Bill Alexander—and it was true.

For many Americans, Ronald Reagan always had seemed larger than life. For years, as a young Hollywood movie actor, Reagan had captured their imaginations as they watched him on the silver screen. Turning to politics in middle age, he expressed the ideas and concerns of a broad range of Americans. Now, after surviving an assassin's bullet, Reagan set out to change the course of United States history.

Above: Spectators hold vigil in the rain outside the hospital.
Below: Congressmen and other officials after visiting Reagan in the hospital

Chapter 2

"Dutch" Reagan

A deep snow clogged the streets of little Tampico, Illinois, on February 6, 1911. Through the frozen drifts Jack Reagan hurried to alert a local doctor and a midwife that his wife was about to have a baby. During the next tense hours Reagan paced about the family apartment above the Pitney General Store. When he finally heard the loud cries of a newborn baby, he rushed into the bedroom. With pride he gazed at his plump, ten-pound infant son and remarked, "For such a little bit of a Dutchman, he makes a hell of a lot of noise, doesn't he?"

"I think he's perfectly wonderful," his wife weakly answered. "Ronald Wilson Reagan." Through the next days Jack Reagan bragged about his "fat little Dutchman." Before long, friends and neighbors referred to young Ronald Reagan by the nickname "Dutch."

The boy's father, John "Jack" Reagan, was a first-generation Irish American. Dutch Reagan later remembered his father as "a handsome man—tall, swarthy, and muscular. . . ." At times Jack Reagan worked as a salesman and manager in various shoe departments and shoe stores. Sadly, though, bad luck and a hopeless drinking problem ruined his chances for a successful career.

Opposite page: Reagan's high-school yearbook photo   15

The Reagans in 1913: Jack, Neil, Ronald, and Nelle

Reagan's mother, Nelle Wilson Reagan, was a small, lovely woman with auburn hair and blue eyes. "She was the gentlest woman, the kindest woman that anyone ever knew," Dutch once declared. Jack Reagan's failure to hold a job forced the family to move from town to town. Everywhere the Reagans lived in Illinois—in Chicago, Galesburg, and Monmouth—Nelle Reagan performed works of neighborhood charity. "We were poor," Reagan later explained, ". . . [but] in those days, you didn't feel poor. . . . There was always someone worse off. My mother was always finding people to help."

Dutch first revealed his adventurous spirit when he was only three. In the summer heat, he and his older brother Neil decided to get a chunk of ice from an ice wagon standing outside the Tampico railroad station. To reach the wagon, Dutch recalled, "my brother and I crawled under a train snorting steam in the station." The boys just reached safety as the chugging train's mighty wheels rolled forward down the track. After witnessing the frightful scene, Nelle Reagan rushed to the station and gave her boys a good spanking.

Young Dutch loved growing up in small-town Illinois. As boys he and his brother explored the countryside. "We used the hills for roaming in the summer and sledding in the winter," he happily recalled. In 1919 the Reagan family moved back to Tampico, where Jack managed Pitney's General Store. Nelle joined a local drama club, and sometimes Dutch sat in the audience at rehearsals. More than anything, though, playing football was his greatest fun. "There was no field, no lines, no goal," he remembered. "Simply grass, the ball, and a mob of excited youngsters."

Although poor, the Reagans took care to provide their sons with a good education. Even before he entered school, Dutch recalled, "my mother took the time to sit down every night and read books to us, following each word with a finger, while we watched over her shoulder." Before the age of five Dutch suddenly realized he could read, too. "One evening all the funny black marks on paper clicked into place," he marveled. As he grew older he excitedly borrowed adventure and sports books from the library.

Ronald Reagan's elementary class photo (he is second row, left)

In December 1920 the Reagan family packed their first car, an old secondhand model, and left Tampico. Jack Reagan had accepted a position in partnership with his boss, H. C. Pitney. In Dixon, Illinois, ninety miles west of Chicago, he would manage the Fashion Boot Shop. Excitedly the Reagan boys helped carry suitcases and boxes into their new rented house at 816 South Hennepin Avenue. Through the center of the pretty town flowed the Rock River. "That river . . . became a great part of my life," Dutch revealed. "In the winter, I loved ice skating on it and in the summer I enjoyed canoeing and swimming there. I hiked along its shores, climbed its limestone bluffs, and went tramping around, exploring the wooded

Ronald Reagan
at the age of 12
in Dixon, Illinois

country nearby." As a special hobby Dutch collected birds'
eggs. "He was always climbing trees to get them," remembered his brother Neil.

Only Jack Reagan's tragic alcoholism ruined his son's
complete joy growing up in Dixon. "I was eleven years
old," Dutch later explained, "the first time I came home to
find my father flat on his back on the front porch. . . . He
was drunk, dead to the world. . . . I felt myself fill with
grief for my father . . . his hair soaked with melting snow,
snoring as he breathed. . . . I bent over him, smelling the
sharp odor of whiskey . . . I managed to drag him inside
and get him to bed. In a few days, he was the bluff, hearty
man I knew and loved, and will always remember."

At school Dutch learned his lessons easily. Unless he saw things close, however, they often seemed very blurred. "I sat in the front row at school," he confessed, "and still could not read the blackboard." One day when he was thirteen he curiously tried on his mother's glasses. "Putting them on, I suddenly saw a glorious, sharply outlined world jump into focus," he recalled. "For the first time, a tree wasn't just a green blob. I could actually see the leaves." With new glasses to correct his nearsightedness, Dutch soon gazed with excitement at the Friday night cliff-hangers and Westerns shown at the local movie theater.

When he entered North Dixon High School in the fall of 1924, Dutch yearned to play on the football team. Because he stood just five feet, three inches tall and weighed only 106 pounds, however, the coach kept him sitting on the bench during games. Dutch could not wait to grow bigger. That summer he found a job working on a construction crew. Swinging a pick for thirty-five cents an hour built muscles on his body. He also took part in the YMCA swimming program and became an expert swimmer.

"The next summer," Dutch recalled, "I got a job I was to keep for seven summers; that of lifeguard at Lowell Park." Reagan suddenly found himself the center of attention. With each passing summer he grew stronger, more handsome, and more confident. "He was the perfect specimen of an athlete, tall, willowy, muscular, brown, good-looking," remembered boyhood friend Bill Thompson. "Of course, the girls were always flocking around him." Dutch took an interest in Margaret Cleaver, the local minister's daughter, and soon they became sweethearts.

The tragedy of several drownings had threatened to close Lowell Park before Reagan became lifeguard. For eighteen dollars a week and all the root beer and hamburgers he could eat at the park snack bar, Reagan protected the bathers. Many times, he spotted swimmers struggling in the river. Plunging into the current, he would swim out and pull them to safety. During the first summer, Jack Reagan suggested that his son cut a notch on an old park log to mark every person he rescued from drowning. At the end of his last lifeguarding season in 1933, park visitors could count seventy-seven notches. Citizens proudly spoke of Dutch Reagan as a local hero.

The teenager also made his mark as he advanced through high school. Gaining height and weight, he played right guard on the football team, shot hoops on the basketball team, and kicked up cinders on the track team. Margaret Cleaver often performed as a member of the high-school drama club. Soon Dutch joined, too, and acted the leading roles in several plays. Elected senior class president, Reagan greatly enjoyed his years in high school. Beside his yearbook picture the caption read, "Life is just one grand sweet song, so start the music."

Dutch dreamed of attending college. Margaret Cleaver had chosen to enter Eureka College in Eureka, Illinois, about eighty miles south of Dixon. In the fall of 1928 Reagan also traveled there. Excitedly he walked among the ivy-covered brick buildings of the lovely little campus. "I fell head over heels in love with Eureka," he afterwards declared. "I wanted to get in that school so badly that it hurt when I thought about it."

Reagan (front, third from left) with his Eureka College fraternity

Room, board, and tuition would use up his four hundred dollars in savings in just one year. Impressed by Reagan's enthusiasm, however, the dean of students granted him an athletic scholarship to cover half of his tuition. To scrape together the rest of the money Reagan took on a number of campus jobs. At his fraternity house, Tau Kappa Epsilon, he rolled up his sleeves and washed dishes after meals. At a girls' dormitory he waited on tables. He also sometimes helped the college groundskeepers rake leaves and shovel snow from sidewalks.

In the classroom Reagan majored in sociology and economics. Years later he admitted, though, "I let football and other . . . activities eat into my study time, with the result that my grade average was closer to the C level . . . than it was to straight A's." As a member of the Eureka football team, Reagan was sometimes clumsy on the field because of his poor eyesight. He loved the game, however, and eventually his determination won him opportunities to play. Reagan showed his school spirit in other ways, too. He reported stories for the student newspaper and helped edit the college yearbook. At basketball games he roused his classmates as a cheerleader, and he was student council president in his senior year.

During his college years, Reagan was perhaps most influenced by his public speaking and dramatics opportunities. When the college president announced financial cutbacks, Eureka students went on strike to save professors' jobs and keep courses open. At a rally, Reagan led the protest with a speech that brought his listeners to their feet with wild cheers. On another night, Reagan attended a play, *Journey's End*. The production deeply moved him, especially the performance of the leading actor. "More than anything in life," he later revealed, "I wanted to speak his lines." As a member of the college drama club, Reagan found he liked acting more and more.

By the end of his senior year, different interests caused Reagan and Margaret Cleaver to drift apart, and in time their long romance ended. There was no question, though, that Reagan's cheerfulness and zest made him a favorite throughout the school. "Everyone admired Dutch," recalled classmate Stanfield Major. "I can't think of anyone who disliked him." In June 1932 Reagan graduated from Eureka. As he collected his diploma, few people knew Reagan seriously hoped somehow to break into show business. Bidding his friends good-bye, he joked, "If I'm not making five thousand a year when I'm five years out of college, I'll consider these four years here wasted."

Chapter 3

The Rising Hollywood Star

"I was broke and in debt," Reagan admitted after leaving college. The great Wall Street stock crash of October 1929 had brought hardship to millions of Americans. As the nation sank into depression, the Reagan family suffered badly. In Dixon the Fashion Boot Shop closed, and Jack Reagan struggled to find jobs as a shoe salesman. The family moved into a cheaper rental house, and Nelle Reagan found work as a seamstress in a local dress shop.

Although he longed to become an actor, Reagan understood his difficult situation. "Broadway was a thousand miles away . . . and Hollywood was two thousand miles . . . and what could I do?" he sadly recalled. "I got to thinking: Radio was relatively new and sports announcing had become something tremendous in a very short time. . . . Finally I conceived the idea, 'Gee, radio sports announcing might lead me where I wanted to go.' "

After finishing his last summer as a lifeguard, the twenty-one-year-old college graduate journeyed to Chicago full of hope. For a week he knocked on the doors at radio stations with no luck. "No one in the city wants to take a chance on inexperience," an NBC receptionist finally told him. She suggested he try some smaller, rural stations.

Opposite page: Ronald Reagan as a
young Warner Brothers actor

Borrowing his father's car, Reagan drove west to the small city of Davenport, Iowa. At radio station WOC, Reagan revealed to station manager Peter MacArthur his desire to become a sports announcer. "Do ye think ye could tell me about a game and make me see it?" the old Scotsman asked. In the station's broadcasting studio, Reagan soon proved that he could. Gripping the microphone, for twenty minutes he expertly reported the play-by-play action of an imaginary football game. "I battled them back and forth, exchanged kicks, and kept watching the clock to make it come out long enough," Reagan later explained.

Greatly impressed, MacArthur hired the young man to announce four University of Iowa football games that fall for ten dollars a game. Reagan never forgot his first thrilling performance as a professional announcer. "My folks had everyone in Dixon listening to the Iowa game that day," he proudly recalled. As friends and neighbors sat beside their radios they heard Dutch Reagan's familiar voice. "How do you do, ladies and gentlemen," he began. "We are speaking to you from high atop the Memorial Stadium of the University of Iowa. . . ."

Reagan showed himself such a smooth and colorful sportscaster that in January 1933 MacArthur hired him as a regular staff announcer at WOC for one hundred dollars a month. Suddenly he had money with which to help his family and a job he truly loved. Through the next months Reagan played records, read commercials, and reported sports events. In April he received a transfer to WOC's larger sister station, WHO, in Des Moines, Iowa. As chief sports announcer at WHO, Reagan broadcast prizefights, track meets, and Big Ten football games.

Listeners who tuned to WHO to hear Chicago Cubs major league baseball games enjoyed Reagan's exciting play-by-play descriptions. They never guessed he was not actually reporting from the baseball stadium in Chicago. Instead, while sitting in the Des Moines studio, Reagan received telegraph messages from the ballpark press box after every play and used his imagination to expand them.

One day during a close Cubs game, the telegraph operator slipped Reagan an unpleasant note: "The wire has gone dead." Rather than stop the broadcast in the middle of the game, Reagan thought fast and described the batter hitting a foul ball. While still out of touch with the ballpark, the young sportscaster kept the batter fouling again and again. "He fouled one back into the box seats" Reagan remembered. "I described in detail the redheaded kid who had scrambled and gotten the souvenir ball. He fouled one into the upper deck that just missed being a home run. He fouled for six minutes and forty-five seconds until I lost count." At last the telegraph wire clicked on again. Reagan's lively imagination had gotten him through.

For recreation Reagan took up horseback riding. Galloping across the Iowa countryside and jumping fences thrilled him. In order to ride for free, a friend suggested Reagan enlist as a reserve officer in the 14th Cavalry Regiment stationed in Des Moines. With his poor vision, Reagan had to cheat to pass the eye exam. He passed his riding test, however, with honest skill and won a second lieutenant's commission in the army reserves.

Reagan the radio announcer
at WOC in Davenport, Iowa
(above) and WHO in Des
Moines, Iowa (left)

During his four years at WHO, Reagan's desire to become an actor never dimmed. In 1937 the Chicago Cubs traveled to Santa Catalina Island, California, for spring training. Seizing the opportunity, Reagan coaxed WHO to let him accompany the team and cover their activities. While in Catalina, the young sportscaster visited nearby Los Angeles and some of the Hollywood motion picture studios. Joy Hodges, an old friend from Des Moines, was a singer in the Jimmy Grier Band and had acted in some movies. Reagan confessed to her that he longed to be an actor.

"I asked him to stand up and remove his glasses," recalled Hodges, "he did, and it was clear that he was VERY HANDSOME. I told him never to put those glasses on again. The next morning I called my agent and Dutch went to see him."

Reagan impressed George Ward of the Meiklejohn Agency with his clean-cut, all-American looks and likable personality. Ward immediately telephoned Warner Brothers studio. Max Arnow, the Warner Brothers casting director, agreed to give Reagan a screen test to see if he possessed the acting ability to appear in movies.

The next Tuesday morning Reagan arrived at Warner Brothers prepared to perform a scene from Philip Barry's play *Holiday*. Reagan remembered that, "with the assistance of a starlet, and with the kindly help of a fine director, I did the scene."

George Ward pleaded with Reagan to stay a few days in Hollywood until studio chief Jack Warner could view the test film.

Reagan, however, had responsibilities. "No," he firmly answered. "I will be on the train tomorrow — me and the Cubs are going home." Fearing he had ruined his Hollywood chances, Reagan journeyed home to Des Moines. On March 22, though, he eagerly tore open a telegram from Ward: "WARNERS OFFER CONTRACT SEVEN YEARS, ONE YEAR'S OPTION, STARTING AT $200 A WEEK. WHAT SHALL I DO?" Completely thrilled, Reagan quickly wired back: "SIGN BEFORE THEY CHANGE THEIR MINDS."

Excitedly Reagan quit his job at WHO, bought a sporty convertible, and drove west to California. Within days of his arrival in Los Angeles, the twenty-six-year-old walked through the gates at Warner Brothers. Hairdressers and makeup artists buzzed about Reagan as they prepared him for his first movie role. With his thick brown hair and clear blue eyes, the six-foot, one-inch Reagan was good-looking. If he could act, Warner Brothers executives believed he had a chance to become a star.

In those days the major Hollywood studios produced both low-budget "B" pictures and more expensive "A" pictures. For his first role, Reagan was cast in the romantic lead of a B picture called *Love Is on the Air*. Playing the part of a fast-talking radio newscaster came naturally to Reagan. In one scene he rushed to a telephone and yelled to his boss, "I've got a story that will crack this town wide open!" The film took only three weeks to shoot. During that time Reagan learned how to move naturally in front of a camera, and his quick ability to memorize lines surprised his fellow actors.

Reagan on a Warner Brothers movie set

Through his first eleven months in Hollywood Reagan performed in eight movies, including brief supporting roles in a few A pictures. It was as a star in B pictures, though, that moviegoers came to know him best. In several films he played the role of Secret Service agent Lieutenant Brass Bancroft. "These were action pictures," remembered Reagan. "I fought in prisons. . . . I fought in an airplane. . . . I swam with . . . bullets, hitting the water six inches from my face."

Ronald Reagan and Jane Wyman in their wedding finery

Directors liked working with Reagan because he always showed up on the set on time and followed their instructions without argument. Reagan posed for hours for publicity photographs, escorted Warner Brothers starlets to movie premieres, and did everything required of a rising movie star. As his success grew, he sent for his parents and bought them a house in Los Angeles. Jack Reagan proudly accepted a job at Warner Brothers—answering the sacks of fan mail that arrived for his movie-star son.

In 1938 the studio cast Reagan in its movie *Brother Rat*. In this successful comedy he played one of three cadets at the Virginia Military Institute. Also appearing in *Brother Rat* was a pretty actress named Jane Wyman. At the time Wyman was divorcing her first husband, Myron Futterman. After the divorce, Reagan revealed his interest in the charming young woman and they began to date.

"When he took me out to dinner," remembered Wyman, ". . . we always seemed to receive special consideration. . . . That was because his manner was as kind, as friendly when he spoke to a waiter as it was when he spoke to a friend." As their romance blossomed she revealed, "I trusted Ronnie. For the first time in my life I truly trusted someone." Gossip columnists and movie fan magazines closely reported the progress of their courtship. Warner Brothers even sent them on a publicity tour around the country. At last, at the Wee Kirk O' Heather Church in Glendale, California, twenty-eight-year-old Ronald Reagan and twenty-six-year-old Jane Wyman exchanged wedding vows. Happily the newlyweds settled into Wyman's Hollywood apartment.

During 1939 and 1940 Reagan accepted leading roles in a long line of Warner Brothers B pictures. When he received smaller parts in A pictures, he jumped at the chance to work with the studio's biggest stars. In the melodrama *Dark Victory* he acted with Bette Davis and Humphrey Bogart. In the historical adventure *Santa Fe Trail*, he played the part of George Custer while Errol Flynn took the larger role of young J. E. B. Stuart.

In 1940 Reagan learned that Warner Brothers planned to produce a movie about famous Notre Dame University football coach Knute Rockne. More than anything, Reagan wanted to play the role of George Gipp, Rockne's most famous player. For days he pestered producer Hal Wallis, hoping for a chance. Finally, after he showed Wallis some convincing photographs of himself in his Eureka College football uniform, he won the part.

In this football movie George Gipp falls deathly ill, and Coach Rockne hurries to visit him. During the filming of the classic hospital deathbed scene, Reagan weakly whispered to actor Pat O'Brien: "Someday, when things are tough, maybe you can ask the boys to go in there and win just once for the Gipper." The film *Knute Rockne— All American* opened in September 1940 to rave reviews, and Reagan's touching performance moved many audiences to tears.

Warner Brothers executives soon rewarded Reagan with an important role in its A picture *Kings Row*. In this 1942 drama Reagan portrayed a character named Drake McHugh. Injured in a train accident, McHugh awakens to discover his legs have been needlessly amputated by a cruel doctor. For the filming of this key scene Reagan climbed into a bed with holes cut through the mattress to hide his legs. For an hour he tensely lay here, imagining the horror of losing his legs. At last the director called, "Action!" "I opened my eyes dazedly, looked around, slowly let my gaze travel downward," Reagan later recalled. "I can't describe even now my feeling as I tried to reach for where my legs should be." In a sweat, he finally screamed his line, "Where's the rest of me?"

Reagan's powerful performance in *Kings Row* won him greater attention than ever before. At last it seemed he was on the verge of real movie stardom. His new agents promptly negotiated a better contract for him at Warner Brothers. Now he earned the giant sum of $1,628 a week. With the birth of his daughter Maureen that same year, Reagan could not have been happier.

Right: Reagan plays George Gipp in *Knute Rockne — All American*

Below: Reagan and actress Ann Sheridan in *Kings Row*

On December 7, 1941, though, world events suddenly interrupted Reagan's life. That Sunday morning bombs exploded, sirens wailed, and stunned sailors dived for cover, as squads of Japanese planes bombed the U.S. naval base at Pearl Harbor, Hawaii. Outraged Americans demanded revenge for the sneak attack, and Congress immediately declared war, thrusting the United States into World War II.

As he was a reserve cavalry officer, thirty-one-year-old Reagan was soon called to active duty. In April 1942 he reported for duty at Fort Mason, California. Required to take a physical exam, Reagan could not hide his weak eyesight. "If we sent you overseas," one examining doctor exclaimed, "you'd shoot a general." "Yes," chimed in another doctor, "and you'd miss him."

Barred from combat, Second Lieutenant Reagan soon received orders to report to the Hal Roach movie studio in Culver City near Los Angeles. The U.S. Army Air Corps had chosen him to become part of its First Motion Picture Unit. In his first assignment at "Fort Roach," Reagan narrated an Army Air Corps film called *Rear Gunner*. This thirty-minute training film helped cut the training period for aerial gunners by six weeks.

Reagan and other officers also studied thousands of feet of combat bomber film, searching for the most successful bombing techniques and making valuable recommendations. On one studio set, special-effects men built a complete model of Tokyo, Japan. Photographed from above, it looked exactly like that enemy city. To train pilots for Tokyo bombing attacks, Fort Roach provided pre-flight

Lieutenant Reagan, daughter Maureen, and wife Jane Wyman in 1942

training films narrated by Reagan. "My voice, as briefing officer, would be heard above the sound of the plane motors," he remembered. In each film he guided the flyers to their targets and then said, "Bombs away."

At last in August 1945 the war did end. Atomic bombs dropped on Hiroshima and Nagasaki forced Japan into complete surrender. For his dedicated service, Reagan eventually was mustered out of the army with the rank of captain. "By the time I got out of the Army Air Corps," Reagan later wrote, "all I wanted to do . . . was rest up awhile . . . love . . . my wife, and come up refreshed to a better job in an ideal world."

Chapter 4

From Actor to Politician

Captain Ronald Reagan returned to civilian life hopefully enough. He and Jane Wyman had adopted a baby boy named Michael in March 1945 to add to their happy family. His agents had bargained on his behalf with Warner Brothers, and soon he was earning the fantastic sum of $3,500 a week. In the spring of 1946 Reagan started acting in a production called *Stallion Road*, "a story of two men, a woman, and a whole herd of beautiful horses." Reagan enjoyed working with horses so much that afterwards as a hobby he bought an expensive horse ranch north of Los Angeles.

As a board member of the Screen Actors Guild (SAG) since 1941, Reagan also took a greater interest in political activities. A union of Hollywood's actors, SAG fought with the movie studios to win better contracts for its members. National politics also held Reagan's interest. In the aftermath of World War II, the Soviet Union was forcing its harsh communist influence upon the countries of Eastern Europe. In China, Mao Tse-tung led a communist revolution. Many Americans feared the rising tide of communism threatened their way of life.

Repeatedly Reagan spoke out against the evils of communism, and he worked hard to keep communist influences out of Hollywood. Many now view this episode in American history as a witch-hunt, an over-reaction to Americans' fears. But SAG members were impressed by Reagan's stand. They elected him their president in March 1947, a position he held for the next six years.

Reagan's interest in union activities and politics may have hurt his acting career. In 1947 he starred in *That Hagan Girl*, a drama that featured Shirley Temple in her first adult role. The movie failed at the box office, though. At the same time, people jammed the doors to see Jane Wyman's latest pictures. In films like *The Yearling* and *The Lost Weekend* she proved herself a serious actress. For her performance as a deaf-mute in the movie *Johnny Belinda*, she carried away an Oscar for best actress at the 1948 Academy Awards ceremonies.

As Reagan and Wyman spent less time together, their marriage suffered. Finally the strain of work pressures and different interests split them apart, and Wyman filed for divorce. In court she testified, "In recent months my husband and I engaged in continual arguments on his political views . . . finally, there was nothing in common between us . . . nothing to sustain our marriage." On June 29, 1948, the court granted the divorce and awarded Wyman custody of their daughter and son. The divorce left thirty-seven-year-old Reagan stunned. "I suppose there had been warning signs," he later remarked. "If only I hadn't been so busy, but small-town boys grow up thinking only other people get divorced. . . ."

Above: Reagan testifying about communist influences in Hollywood before the House Committee on Un-American Activities

Right: Jane Wyman kisses the Oscar she was awarded as best actress of 1948.

To forget his pain, Reagan accepted parts in a number of Warner Brothers films. In time Reagan agreed to a new contract that allowed him to make movies at other studios as well. At Universal Pictures in 1951 he acted the role of a college professor trying to raise a chimpanzee in the comedy *Bedtime for Bonzo.* Jumping about in every scene, the cute chimpanzee Bonzo easily stole the show. Years later someone showed Reagan a photograph from the movie, picturing him in bed with Bonzo. "I'm the one with the watch," Reagan laughed. None of his movies during these years, however, did much to boost his acting career.

Reagan remained fully involved with the Screen Actors Guild. He had many actor friends and he dated beautiful Hollywood starlets. Still he felt unhappy. "My loneliness was not from being unloved, but rather from not loving," he remembered. "I wanted to care for someone."

One day late in 1949 Reagan's telephone rang. Director Mervyn Le Roy explained that he knew a young actress named Nancy Davis. Her name kept appearing against her will on the rosters of several Hollywood organizations that were considered friendly toward communism. In those politically troubled times, she was concerned about her career. As president of the Screen Actors Guild, Reagan straightened out the problem and agreed to meet with her. On a pleasant California evening he arrived at Nancy Davis's apartment. "The door opened," he recalled, "not on the expected fan magazine version of a starlet, but on a small, slender young lady with dark hair and a wide-spaced pair of hazel eyes that looked right at you and made you look back."

Born Anne Francis Robbins on July 6, 1923, Nancy Davis had begun her acting career after graduating from Smith College. She took her stage name from her nickname Nancy and her stepfather's last name, Davis. That night Reagan escorted her to dinner and a nightclub. He found her lively, attractive, and intelligent and enjoyed her company so much that they stayed out until 3:30 A.M.

Through the next two years the couple dated until Reagan fully realized he had fallen in love. Finally one night he sat at a SAG meeting with his good friend actor William Holden. On a pad he suddenly scribbled a note: "To hell with this, how would you like to be best man when I marry Nancy?" "It's about time!" blurted out Holden. At the age of forty-one Ronald Reagan married twenty-eight-year-old Nancy Davis on March 4, 1952. After the simple service at the Little Brown Church in California's San Fernando Valley, the loving couple honeymooned in Phoenix, Arizona.

Although his private life had reached a state of perfect happiness, Reagan's screen career kept slowly sliding downward. In 1952 he finished his last picture for Warner Brothers. *The Winning Team*, the life story of baseball pitcher Grover Cleveland Alexander, won Reagan fine reviews. His next few roles, however, were in low-budget films that flopped at the box office. While he waited for a role that would bolster his sagging star status, Reagan rejected three weak film scripts in a row. Income taxes swallowed a large chunk of his savings. Out of work for fourteen months, by the start of 1954 Reagan suddenly found himself $18,000 in debt.

Above: "I'm the one with the watch," quipped Reagan of this shot from
Bedtime for Bonzo. Below: Ronald and Nancy cut their wedding cake.
With them are actor William Holden and his wife, actress Brenda Marshall.

Reagan and the Continentals at Las Vegas's Last Frontier Hotel

In despair, the actor agreed to perform for two weeks in a Las Vegas nightclub act. As the master of ceremonies, Reagan joined a male quartet called The Continentals in songs, dances, and comedy skits. The work paid him $30,000, and audiences loudly applauded the entertaining show. As a professional actor, though, Reagan was sure he had hit rock bottom. In embarrassment he afterwards declared, "Never again will I sell myself so short."

At last in the summer of 1954 an opportunity arrived that would change Reagan's life. The General Electric Company chose him to host its half-hour television show "The General Electric Theater." Starting at a salary of $125,000 a year, Reagan introduced the dramas and comedies that CBS studios broadcast every Sunday night. He also starred in some of the teleplays, and "GE Theater" became an instant winner.

Reagan's duties with General Electric included personal appearance tours. He never forgot his visit to his first General Electric plant. As he strode onto the factory floor he remembered, "Machines went untended or ground to a halt; the aisles filled with men and women bearing their children's autograph books."

Through the next eight years as a traveling goodwill ambassador, Reagan journeyed to 135 General Electric plants and met about 250,000 GE employees. The exhausting work often left his feet blistered and his fingers sore from shaking hands.

During his tours Reagan gladly told stories about Hollywood and his work. Soon he expanded his daily talks to cover other subjects as well. "You'd better get yourself a philosophy," GE chairman Ralph Cordiner suggested to him. "Something you can stand for and something you think this country stands for." The philosophy Reagan easily chose was that of a political conservative. Soon he developed a regular speech that praised private enterprise and complained about government interference.

As Reagan's success grew, he and Nancy built a dream house in Pacific Palisades, California. General Electric filled the house with every imaginable electrical gadget that they made. In 1957 Ron and Nancy took time to star in a film together, their only joint movie appearance. In *Hellcats of the Navy* Reagan played a World War II submarine officer on a dangerous mission. Nancy Reagan retired from films the next year after giving birth to a son. Little Ronald Prescott Reagan joined his sister Patti, who had been born in 1952, at the cheerful Reagan home.

**Above: Reagan, Nancy, and actor
Arthur Franz in the 1957 movie
*Hellcats of the Navy***

**Right: The Reagans with daughter
Patti and son Ronald Prescott**

In 1962 CBS finally canceled "General Electric Theater." That year "NBC moved TV's top-rated show, *Bonanza*, from its Saturday spot to Sunday," Reagan explained, "and . . . we ran second most of the time." Having reached middle age, Reagan searched for other roles to play. Moviegoers next saw him playing a crime lord in the 1964 film *The Killers*. He had never played a villain before, and the unusual role marked his fifty-third and last movie appearance. To stay in the public eye, the aging actor accepted the part of the host on the television show "Death Valley Days." Standing in the desert, he introduced twenty-one episodes of that western series starting in 1965.

As his acting career once more faded, Reagan turned more and more to politics. In 1960 he had delivered two hundred campaign speeches in behalf of Republican presidential candidate Richard Nixon, who nevertheless lost the election. Four years later he campaigned even harder when Republican Barry Goldwater ran for president against Lyndon Johnson in 1964. As cochairman of the California Republicans for Goldwater organization, Reagan stumped across the state praising Goldwater's conservative beliefs.

To help raise money for Goldwater, Reagan filmed a thirty-minute appeal. The speech, called "A Time for Choosing," aired on national television on October 27, 1964. "You and I have a rendezvous with destiny," Reagan declared to viewers across the country. "We can preserve for our children this last best hope of man on earth, or we can sentence them to take the first step into a thousand years of darkness." Using all of his skills as an actor,

Reagan at a press conference during his campaign for California governor

Reagan electrified his audience. Although Goldwater lost the election one week later, Reagan's address drew one million dollars in Republican contributions, more than any other single political speech in American history.

Overnight, conservative Republicans recognized Reagan as a hero of their cause. Wealthy California conservatives soon urged him to run for governor in 1966. At first Reagan refused to consider the idea. "No way," he exclaimed. "You find a candidate and I'll campaign for him." Flattered by their constant entreaties, however, he finally agreed to run.

Chapter 5

Reagan of California

In January 1966 fifty-four-year-old Ronald Reagan plunged into California politics as a candidate for governor. A committee of wealthy "Friends of Ronald Reagan" supported his campaign. Through the next months he crisscrossed the state, meeting the people and learning the issues. Naturally Reagan appeared at his best during TV appearances. Looking healthy and relaxed, he appealed to Californians with plain and touching language. On June 2 his skill as a communicator easily won him the Republican nomination.

The general election pitted Reagan against popular Democratic governor Edmund "Pat" Brown. Brown failed to take Reagan very seriously. "While I was working for this state, as district attorney, attorney general, and for the last eight years as governor, what was my opponent doing?" exclaimed Brown. "Well, he was making movies like . . . *Bedtime for Bonzo*. Can you imagine turning over this great state to that actor?"

Opposite page: Campaigning for governor   51

Reagan in turn attacked Brown's record. Calling himself a "citizen-politician" he promised to cut taxes and government wastefulness if elected. "Vote for me," he declared, "if you believe as I do that we have here within our borders the greatest people in all this nation and all this earth. . . . There isn't anything that we cannot do if we are given a chance to do it."

On election day, November 8, 1966, Californians made their choice. By an astonishing vote of 3,742,913 to 2,749,174, the actor Ronald Reagan won the right to sit in the California governor's chair.

On the night of January 2, 1967, people crowded into the state capitol in Sacramento to witness Reagan's inauguration. Another former actor, U.S. senator from California George Murphy, led the procession into the capitol rotunda. "Well, George, here we are on the Late Show again," teased Reagan after taking the oath of office.

As he undertook the important job before him, Governor Reagan discovered with dismay that the California state treasury was $194 million in debt. Quickly he moved to cure the problem. He instructed all state agencies to cut their budgets by 10 percent and ordered a freeze on the hiring of new state workers. Cutting corners everywhere, Reagan gained a reputation for thriftiness. Instead of buying new paper and envelopes, for example, Reagan told statehouse secretaries just to cross out Pat Brown's name and type in his own.

At regular Tuesday morning press conferences, Governor Reagan answered questions with charm and skill. He also showed his mastery at public relations by taping a regular series of two-minute televised "Reports to the People" on state issues. Some Californians grinned when they learned of Reagan's habit at cabinet meetings. Having quit smoking, the governor found he enjoyed chewing on jelly beans as a substitute. On the cabinet room table he placed a large jar of the colorful candies, which he generously passed around during sessions. "We can hardly start a meeting or make a decision," he joked, "without passing around the jar of jelly beans."

As governor, Reagan ran the state as the chairman of a large corporation would. After stating his general desires, he allowed his aides and department heads to carry out his policies.

Reagan's failure to study every detail of state business caused his enemies to label him "the *acting* governor." Still, he successfully dealt with a number of important California matters. Although he had promised to cut taxes, Reagan signed a new billion-dollar tax increase to help balance the state budget. Corporate, personal, and sales taxes were raised, but he lowered property taxes, which often burdened elderly homeowners.

Confusion swept through many of California's colleges in the late 1960s. Upset about American participation in the Vietnam War, mobs of students marched and protested. When rioting and destruction occurred at some colleges Reagan acted swiftly. Repeatedly he called upon state troopers and national guardsmen to stop campus violence. "This administration," warned Reagan, "will do whatever is possible to maintain order on our campuses. . . . I don't care what force it takes. That force must be applied."

Californians who admired Reagan's politics voted him a second term in office in 1970. Eight years in California's statehouse earned Reagan fame as a national political figure. Conservative Republicans throughout the country regarded him as their most effective spokesman and wished to make him president. In 1968 Reagan received 182 delegate votes at the Republican national convention. Republicans that year, however, nominated Richard Nixon, who had been their candidate in 1960. "Son," South Carolina senator Strom Thurmond told Reagan, "you'll be President some day, but this isn't your year."

As the 1976 national election approached, former governor Reagan thought perhaps his time had come. Scandal rocked the White House during Richard Nixon's second term as president. Nixon's attempts to cover up White House involvement in the famous Watergate burglary outraged most Americans. On the verge of impeachment, Nixon shamefully resigned his office on August 9, 1974. Suddenly Vice-President Gerald Ford had found himself thrust into the presidency.

Some Republicans worried that Ford would not be a strong enough candidate to win the 1976 election. Urged on by his conservative friends, on November 21, 1975, Reagan announced his decision to challenge Ford for his party's presidential nomination. Crisscrossing the United States, both Ford and Reagan battled for Republican delegate support. As president during difficult times, Ford had won many people's admiration. To gain support Reagan attacked Ford's foreign policy. He demanded that America meet the growing communist threat of the Soviet Union by

Richard Nixon gives his farewell speech on August 9, 1974.

expanding U.S. military strength and developing more nuclear weapons. Reagan also claimed that President Ford was plotting to give away the valuable Panama Canal, which linked the Atlantic and Pacific Oceans. "When it comes to the Canal," Reagan defiantly declared, "we built it, we paid for it, it's ours, and we should . . . keep it!" Reagan's bold words and fighting spirit roused many Americans' support.

At last in August 1976 the Republican delegates gathered at their national convention in Kansas City, Missouri. Cheers and shouts echoed through the auditorium as their votes were tallied. By the extremely close count of 1,187 to 1,070, Gerald Ford defeated Ronald Reagan for the Republican presidential nomination. "We lost," Reagan conceded to his unhappy conservative supporters, "but the cause—the cause goes on. . . ."

The Democratic candidate, former Georgia governor Jimmy Carter, beat Ford in the 1976 election. Carter encountered many problems while in the White House. The value of the dollar shrank, unemployment rose, and fuel shortages caused cars to line up for hours at gas stations. A foreign crisis erupted in November 1979 in Iran. Muslim revolutionaries attacked the U.S. embassy in that Middle Eastern nation and took fifty-four Americans hostage. As the 1980 election campaign neared, Nevada senator Paul Laxalt openly declared, "At a time of dangerous weakness and confusion in the presidency, Ronald Reagan would provide a welcome change as a 'take charge' President." Many people regarded Reagan as the clear choice for Republican candidate in 1980. "Do you have all the vigor you need for a campaign?" a reporter asked as Reagan approached his sixty-ninth birthday. "Yes," he answered. "The whole issue of my age will be resolved when people see that I can go the distance."

Several other Republicans also hoped to win the nomination. They took every opportunity to attack front-runner Reagan and his conservative remedies for the nation's problems. "The way to fight inflation," Reagan told audiences, "is to whittle down the size of the federal government, remove the layers of fat, and then cut the income taxes across the board for everybody in the country!" Former Central Intelligence Agency (CIA) director George Bush called this plan "voodoo economics," and other critics jokingly referred to it as "Reaganomics." Meeting in political caucuses in January, Iowa Republicans cast their support to George Bush for president.

Above: Jimmy Carter at the 1976
Democratic national convention

Right: Iranian demonstrators
burn an American flag on the
wall of the U.S. embassy in
Teheran after taking 54
American hostages.

In alarm, Reagan doubled his schedule of speeches in New Hampshire, the first state to hold a primary vote to elect convention delegates. Eagerly Reagan agreed to pay the expenses for a public debate with Bush. At one point the host tried to stop Reagan from expressing an opinion. "Will the sound man please turn Mr. Reagan's mike off?" he ordered. The audience cheered, though, as Reagan furiously grabbed the microphone and reminded the host, "I am paying for this microphone!"

Reagan's outspokenness that night and his fiery energy as he traveled the state gained him renewed support. As a result, he won the New Hampshire primary and his campaign rapidly picked up momentum. As the weaker candidates dropped out of the race, Reagan swept one primary contest after another. In July 1980, Republican delegates excitedly gathered for their national convention in Detroit, Michigan, certain that Reagan would be their nominee for president. In the Joe Louis Arena the crowd roared, bands blared, and balloons dropped from the ceiling when the first-ballot vote delivered Reagan's victory. For vice-president on the Republican ticket, Reagan chose his old rival George Bush. Unhappy with the convention's outcome, Illinois congressman John Anderson soon announced he would run for president as an independent candidate.

Democratic delegates nominated Jimmy Carter to run for a second term at their August convention in New York City. The Democrats laughed that a former actor could not possibly perform the duties of president. "Bonzo, Bonzo, Bonzo!" yelled hecklers at one rally to ridicule Reagan's past. "Well, they better watch out," responded Reagan.

"Bonzo grew up to be King Kong!" In fact his past career again proved of great value to Reagan. In interviews and during speeches he communicated with poise, wit, and skillful timing. One Republican media adviser proudly announced that Reagan was "the greatest television candidate in history."

Reagan put his communicating ability to its greatest test during his televised debate with Jimmy Carter on October 28. Reagan's patience and calm attitude won the sympathy of many viewers that night. His closing remarks swayed the opinions of millions of others. "Next Tuesday," he stated, "all of you will go to the polls; you'll stand there . . . and make a decision. I think when you make that decision; it might be well if you would ask yourself: Are you better off than you were four years ago?"

On election day, November 4, 1980, Americans clearly decided that they wanted a change. Carter admitted defeat even before some polling places closed. When the votes were finally counted they revealed:

	Popular Vote	Electoral Vote
Ronald Reagan	43,899,248	489
Jimmy Carter	35,481,435	49
John Anderson	5,719,437	0

By a huge margin, Americans had elected Reagan president of the United States. "It's a great surprise, I just can't believe it," he humbly exclaimed when he heard the news. "I am not frightened by what lies ahead and I don't believe the American people are frightened," he further declared. "Together, we are going to do what has to be done. We're going to put America back to work again."

Chapter 6

The Great Communicator

Thousands of eager citizens packed the streets of Washington, D.C., on January 20, 1981. Near the west front of the Capitol, they jammed shoulder to shoulder to witness Ronald Reagan's swearing-in ceremony. Americans sighed with relief on that cold inauguration day, for just hours earlier, the Iranians had released their U.S. hostages. After 444 days of imprisonment, these American heroes were coming home at last.

The crowd watched excitedly as Reagan, bundled in an overcoat, stepped onto the Capitol platform. Standing before Supreme Court Chief Justice Warren Burger, he repeated the oath of office, vowing to "preserve, protect and defend" the Constitution. At the age of sixty-nine he became fortieth president of the United States, the oldest person ever to win that office.

"Now, so there will be no misunderstanding," he firmly exclaimed in his inaugural address, "it's not my intention to do away with government. It is rather to make it work—work with us, not over us; to stand by our side, not ride on our back." In spite of his age, Americans sensed Reagan would charge ahead to lead the nation with renewed spirit and hope.

Reagan passes a jar of jelly beans to budget director David Stockman.

"There will be jelly beans in the White House, that's all I can say," exclaimed one Reagan supporter. Republicans adopted Reagan's favorite candy as a symbol of the new administration. "Everywhere I go, I see jelly beans," marveled economist Milton Friedman. At cabinet meetings Reagan always kept a jar of jelly beans within reach.

Relying heavily on his staff and his department heads to carry out his orders, Reagan promptly tackled the problem of the nation's weak economy. The Democrats who controlled the House of Representatives prepared to fight all Reaganomics tax-cut proposals. On March 30, 1981, however, a shocking attack on the president interrupted all government business. A crazed assassin named John Hinckley, Jr. fired gunshots at the president outside the Washington Hilton Hotel. Bullets cut down a policeman, a Secret Service agent, and White House press secretary

Actress Jodi Foster (left); John Hinckley, Jr. (right)

James Brady. A fourth bullet smashed against the door frame of Reagan's limousine. The slug bounced off the frame and ripped into his chest, lodging in his left lung.

After he was rushed to nearby George Washington University Hospital, doctors anxiously removed the bullet. Despite his seventy years, Reagan made a speedy recovery and never lost his spirit. "Does anybody know what that guy's beef was?" he later asked about the captured gunman. Stunned Americans soon learned that Hinckley, the son of a wealthy Texas oilman, had drifted about the country for several years. After watching a movie called *Taxi Driver*, about an attempted assassination, he had fallen in love with its young actress Jodi Foster. To show his love for her, Hinckley had madly vowed to kill the president. In time, a court declared Hinckley insane and a judge committed him to a mental institution.

Air traffic controllers on strike in New York

Having survived this senseless assassination attempt, Reagan emerged from the hospital more popular than ever. Few Democrats dared to block his economic proposals now. As a result, Reagan slashed government spending and pushed his tax cuts through Congress. "In 1981," he proudly reminded Americans later, ". . . we cut your tax rates . . . by nearly twenty-five per cent. And what that helped trigger was falling inflation, falling interest rates and the strongest economic expansion in thirty years." This was true, although a serious economic recession in the early 1980s had also helped stop inflation and rising interest rates.

Reagan showed his leadership in other areas as well. In August 1981 some 80 percent of the nation's 15,000 air traffic controllers walked off their jobs. Commercial planes sat idly in airports as these controllers marched in picket lines and demanded better working conditions.

Reagan and Justice Sandra Day O'Connor after her swearing-in ceremony

Reagan quickly vowed not to let the strike paralyze the nation's air transportation system. When many stubborn strikers refused to stop striking, he promptly had them fired. Using military crews, civilian supervisors, and non-striking controllers, Reagan kept many planes flying. Airports slowly returned to normal as newly trained controllers undertook the difficult work.

In July 1981 Americans welcomed Reagan's decision to name Sandra Day O'Connor of Arizona as an associate justice to the United States Supreme Court. O'Connor became the first woman ever to wear the honored black judicial robes in the nation's highest court. Some other Reagan appointments proved less successful. Secretary of the Interior James Watt tried to open government lands to oil drilling and mining operators. Nature lovers insisted that Watt would destroy the nation's wilderness. Under constant attack, Watt finally resigned his post in 1983.

A U.S. Marine stands guard near the bombed-out Beirut Marine headquarters.

Many Americans were also upset about problems in the Environmental Protection Agency and cutbacks in domestic programs. The unemployment rate had reached 11 percent by 1982, and millions of Americans were suffering from a decrease in social services. The national debt was increasing to record levels, too, reaching $110 billion in 1982 and $195 billion in 1983.

Political opponents complained about Reagan's foreign policies as well. In the Middle Eastern nation of Lebanon, Christian and Muslim religious sects had been fighting an ugly civil war. Under Reagan's direction, eight hundred U.S. Marines landed at the Lebanese capital of Beirut in August 1982. Shoveling sandbags and stretching barbed wire, these men dug in near Beirut International Airport as part of an international peacekeeping force.

Some Muslims deeply resented American interference

Memorial service for Marines killed in the Beirut bombing

in Lebanon. At dawn on October 23, 1983, a Muslim terrorist rammed a truck through the fence at the U.S. Marine compound. Sentries watched helplessly as the bomb-filled truck smashed into the main headquarters building. The truck exploded with a deafening roar, and the destroyed building crashed down, killing 241 Marines almost instantly. The image of flag-draped coffins returning from Lebanon sadly pointed out the failure of U.S. peacekeeping efforts there.

Just two days after the disaster in Beirut, Americans suddenly shifted their attention to the little Caribbean island nation of Grenada. Grenada's communist government was in revolt, and visiting Cuban soldiers patroled the streets. The U.S. government feared for the safety of dozens of American students in medical school there. With a growing threat of violence, Reagan acted quickly.

American troops storm inland after landing in Grenada.

At dawn on October 25, 1983, U.S. Marines stormed ashore on Grenada's beaches. Overhead the parachutes of U.S. paratroopers floated down from the sky. This surprise invasion force, totaling 1,900 men, battled communist Grenadian and Cuban army units through the day. Although eighteen American soldiers died during the swift attack, the enemy soon threw up their hands in surrender. The frightened American students trapped in Grenada loudly cheered the arrival of their rescuers. Most Grenadians also thanked the United States for restoring democracy and peace to their country. At the same time, Reagan's critics questioned whether the invasion was necessary, efficient, or good for America's image.

As Reagan advanced through his presidential term, his easy personal warmth, good humor, and real concern about the nation's future won him the hearts of millions of Americans. Whenever the Democrats threatened to fight his programs, Reagan took his message directly to the people. His televised speeches as well as his regular Saturday radio broadcasts, delivered in a plain and convincing style, earned him the nickname "The Great Communicator."

Other Americans, remembering Reagan's famous movie role as football star George Gipp, liked calling him "The Gipper." Even in his seventies the president remained in sturdy health. At the White House he exercised daily, lifting weights and pedaling an exercise bike. For outdoor recreation he still loved riding horses. Often he vacationed at Rancho del Cielo, a 688-acre ranch he had purchased near Santa Barbara, California. In a work shirt and jeans, he cheerfully chopped brush and split wood.

As they pursued their varied careers, Reagan's four grown children sometimes visited the White House. Generally the president preferred to keep his family life private, but it was clear to everyone that he was completely devoted to his wife. Whenever he felt troubled, First Lady Nancy Reagan provided her husband with support. During the 1980s the tragedy of drug and alcohol abuse plagued the United States more than ever before. Deeply concerned, Nancy Reagan taped television and radio appeals. "Say 'yes' to life," she urged young people. "And when it comes to drugs and alcohol, just say 'no.' " Her national "Just Say No" campaign helped steer thousands of youngsters away from the dangers of drugs and alcohol.

VOICE OF AMERICA

THE THRILL CAN KILL

JUST SAY NO TO DRUGS

Above: Reagan making his weekly radio broadcast over Voice of America, which reaches Eastern Europe and the Soviet Union

Left: Nancy Reagan speaking in behalf of her anti-drug campaign

Democratic candidates Geraldine Ferraro and Walter Mondale

By the time the 1984 election neared, Americans enjoyed tremendous prosperity and felt a great sense of national pride under Reagan's leadership. Democrats searched hard to find a candidate to challenge the popular president. At their national convention in San Francisco, California, in July 1984, they finally awarded the nomination to former vice-president Walter Mondale. He picked New York congresswoman Geraldine Ferraro as his vice-presidential running mate. No major U.S. political party ever had chosen a woman for its national ticket before. Ferraro's nomination thrilled many women voters.

Republican delegates stood firmly behind Reagan when in August they convened in Dallas, Texas. Amid glad shouts and waving banners, they unanimously picked Ronald Reagan to run for a second term. To Republicans, the Reagan-Bush ticket simply stood for American patriotism, religious faith, and high family ideals.

Mondale and Reagan shake hands before a television debate.

Although he seemed unbeatable, Reagan still campaigned hard. Everywhere he visited he attacked Mondale's pledge to raise taxes to pay for new government programs. Twice the two candidates met to debate the issues on television. During their first debate seventy-three-year-old Reagan appeared tired and confused. "IS OLDEST U.S. PRESIDENT NOW SHOWING HIS AGE?" blared *The Wall Street Journal* the next day. Stories that Reagan sometimes dozed during cabinet meetings surfaced. It was no secret that the president wore contact lenses to see and hearing aids to correct deafness. To remove doubts about his health and energy, Reagan prepared much more carefully for his second meeting with Mondale. Relaxed and knowledgeable, he performed much better. "I will not make age an issue in this campaign," he jested at one point. "I'm not going to exploit for political purposes my opponent's youth and inexperience."

The Reagans and the Bushes at the 1984 Republican national convention

Through the last days of the election race, Reagan followed a careful schedule and stumped across the country. On November 7, 1984, Americans headed for the polls and voted for their clear choice. The final tally of the votes astonished everyone:

	Popular Vote	Electoral Vote
Ronald Reagan	54,450,603	525
Walter Mondale	37,573,671	13

By the huge popular-vote margin of 59 percent Reagan triumphed. Of the electoral vote, Mondale captured only the District of Columbia and his home state of Minnesota. "Reagan is the most popular figure in the history of the United States," confessed Democratic Speaker of the House Thomas "Tip" O'Neill. "No candidate we put up would have been able to beat Reagan this year."

Chapter 7

One More for the Gipper

At noon on January 20, 1985, Ronald Reagan stood at the foot of the grand staircase in the White House. Inauguration day that year fell on a Sunday. Therefore Reagan took his second oath of office in a simple private ceremony. With his wife at his side holding the family Bible, Reagan stated in a firm voice, "I do solemnly swear that I will faithfully execute the office of President of the United States. . . ."

The next day frigid weather, with temperatures below 10 degrees Fahrenheit, gripped Washington, D.C. For the first time in history, officials abandoned plans for a public outdoor inauguration ceremony and a parade. Instead, in the Capitol rotunda, Reagan repeated his oath before government officials and friends. Then he turned and read his second inaugural address. "Four years ago I spoke to you of a new beginning," he told Americans, "and we have accomplished that. . . . Tax rates have been reduced, inflation cut dramatically and more people are employed than ever before. . . . Let history say of us, these were golden years—when the American Revolution was reborn, when freedom gained new life and America reached for her best. . . ."

Libyan leader Muammar Kaddafi at a 1983 news conference

As Reagan started his second term, troubles with the North African country of Libya soon demanded his attention. For years Libyan dictator Colonel Muammar Kaddafi openly provided Arab terrorist groups with guns and shelter within his country. "By providing material support to terrorist groups which attack U.S. citizens," Reagan angrily announced in December 1985, "Libya has engaged in armed aggression against the United States." On April 5, 1986, a terrorist bomb demolished a West Berlin nightclub often visited by U.S. soldiers. One innocent American serviceman died in the bloody blast.

The French embassy in Tripoli, Libya, after the American bombing raid

On April 15 the United States struck back at Libya with fury. In the early-morning blackness, U.S. fighter-bombers suddenly roared through the sky above the Libyan cities of Tripoli and Benghazi. During their half-hour surprise attack, 2,000-pound bombs rained down on "terrorist-related targets," including the army barracks where Kaddafi lived. Though Kaddafi escaped injury, the raid left the Libyan people stunned. "Today we have done what we had to do," President Reagan afterwards declared. "If necessary, we shall do it again." Though many Americans criticized his stern action, his popularity soared with those who praised his initiative.

U.S. military forces also saw action in the Persian Gulf. When a brutal war between the Middle Eastern nations of Iran and Iraq spilled into the gulf's shipping lanes, the oil tankers that traveled those waters were in danger. Seeing a possible loss of America's oil supply, Reagan sent a U.S. Navy task force to the gulf. On May 17 a missile fired by an Iraqi warplane slammed into the U.S. frigate *Stark*. Americans sadly lowered flags to half-mast when they learned that thirty-seven sailors had died in the tragic accidental attack. "From now on . . . there is one order of battle," instructed the president—"defend yourselves, defend American lives." Only when Iran and Iraq agreed to a ceasefire in the fall of 1988 was calm finally restored to the Persian Gulf.

At home Reagan faced an important personal battle in July 1985. Doctors discovered a tumor two inches long growing on his large intestine. "The president has cancer," gravely revealed Dr. Steven Rosenberg.

Americans waited anxiously for news as Reagan underwent cancer surgery at Bethesda Naval Medical Center in Maryland on July 13. Doctors carefully cut into the president's abdomen and removed a two-foot section of his large intestine. Through the next five days Reagan recovered with surprising speed and doctors announced the complete success of the operation. "The Gipper Is Home!" "The Gipper Comes Through (Again)!" read signs waved by the happy crowd that greeted Reagan on his return to the White House on July 20. "I'm feeling great," grinned the president, "but I'm getting a little restless. I'm eager to get back to work."

Above: A giant hole blown in the side of the USS *Stark* by an Iraqui jet
Below: Reagan waves from his hospital window after his cancer surgery.

Astronauts Sally Ride and Guion Bluford

During Reagan's years in office, the National Aeronautics and Space Administration (NASA) thrilled the nation with advances in America's manned space program. When the first reusable U.S. space shuttle *Columbia* blasted into orbit on April 12, 1981, it signaled the start of a bold new era in spaceflight. Three other shuttles—*Challenger, Discovery,* and *Atlantis*—soon also joined the fleet. Their missions launched communications satellites and conducted valuable space experiments. On its second trip, *Challenger* carried America's first woman into space, Sally Ride. Guion Bluford, the country's first black astronaut, flew on *Challenger*'s third mission.

The *Challenger* crew, from left: Ellison Onizuka, Mike Smith, Christa McAuliffe, Dick Scobee, Greg Jarvis, Ron McNair, and Judy Resnick

On January 28, 1986, *Challenger* was readied for NASA's twenty-fifth shuttle flight. Excited spectators at Cape Canaveral, Florida, took special interest that day because a New Hampshire schoolteacher named Christa McAuliffe had joined *Challenger*'s six crew members. McAuliffe would be the first "citizen observer" to ride a shuttle into space. Its engines blazing and its rockets trailing smoke, *Challenger* thrust up into the sky. Then bystanders cried out with horror as the shuttle suddenly burst in a fireball. A fuel leak caused by a faulty seal had caused *Challenger* to explode into thousands of pieces, killing all seven passengers.

In its twenty-five years of space exploration the United States never had suffered a worse disaster. Through the next mournful days President Reagan tried to comfort shocked Americans. "The crew of the space shuttle *Challenger* honored us by the manner in which they lived their lives," he declared. "We will never forget them nor the last time we saw them . . . as they prepared for their journey and waved goodbye and slipped the surly bonds of earth to touch the face of God. . . . Man will continue his conquest of space, to reach out for new goals and ever greater achievements. That is the way we shall commemorate our seven *Challenger* heroes."

Closer to earth, Reagan faced the greatest crisis of his political career. In the Central American jungles of Nicaragua, rebel soldiers called contras skirmished with the communist troops of Nicaragua's Sandinista government. "There are over 15,000 freedom fighters struggling for liberty and democracy in Nicaragua," exclaimed Reagan in 1985. "They are our brothers. How can we ignore them?" Repeatedly Reagan asked that military aid be sent to the contras. Unwilling to involve the United States in a foreign war, however, Congress passed the Boland Amendment, which banned contra military aid.

At the same time, several U.S. hostages were being held in Lebanon by Muslim terrorists. Although U.S. policy forbade providing arms to terrorists in exchange for hostages, the Reagan administration decided to sell U.S. Hawk missiles and spare missile parts secretly to Iran. After the delivery of this weaponry, the Iranians persuaded the terrorists in Lebanon to release a few of the U.S. hostages.

Oliver North is sworn in before testifying about his contra aid activities.

In November 1986 Americans voiced outrage as news of the secret arms deal leaked. They exploded with deeper anger when they next found out that profits from the arms sales had been used to aid the Nicaraguan contras. Even Reagan seemed surprised by that twist in the story. He promptly ordered a special commission to investigate.

The Iran-contra scandal widened when it was found that Marine Lieutenant Colonel Oliver North, a staff member of the U.S. National Security Council (NSC), was running the secret contra aid operation. At a televised congressional inquiry in July 1987 North admitted secretly funneling money to the contras. He claimed, though, that he was only following orders. "I assumed that the President was aware of what I was doing and had, through my superiors, approved it," he testified. Because he had failed to stop North's activities, NSC chief Vice Admiral John Poindexter resigned his post. White House chief of staff Donald Regan was also forced to resign.

Furious Americans demanded to know what part President Reagan had played in the entire affair. In a televised address Reagan somberly apologized: "When it came to managing the NSC staff, let's face it, my style didn't match my previous track record. . . . As disappointed as I may be in some who served me, I am still the only one who must answer to the American people. . . . I didn't know about any diversion of funds to the contras. But as President I cannot escape responsibility."

The investigations continued, but Americans could not stay mad at the president for long. His efforts to improve U.S. relations with the Soviet Union marked a huge success in foreign affairs. Upon entering the White House Reagan had called the Soviet Union an "evil empire." He accused the Russians of mounting "the greatest military buildup in the history of man." To combat the Soviet threat, Reagan ordered U.S. defense spending to the highest levels ever.

When Mikhail Gorbachev became the vigorous new premier of the Soviet Union in March 1984, Reagan offered to thaw America's cold relations with the USSR. "If the Soviet government wants peace," he declared, "then there will be peace." Immediately Gorbachev agreed to talks. Through the next four years the two world leaders sat together four times at formal summit meetings. "We discussed nuclear arms and how to reduce them," reported Reagan after their first meeting in Geneva, Switzerland. Meetings at Reykjavík, Iceland and Washington, D.C., followed in 1986. "We can get along. We can cooperate," stated Reagan as he grew to know Gorbachev better. In June 1987 Reagan and Gorbachev strolled together in

Gorbachev and Reagan at a ceremony following a summit meeting

Moscow's Red Square. Although the two leaders remained politically opposed, Reagan told reporters, "There is good chemistry between us. I think that through this succession of summits there is a better understanding."

Most important, these U.S.-Soviet meetings resulted in the signing of a historic weapons treaty in 1986. The Intermediate-range Nuclear Forces (INF) Treaty called for the destruction of hundreds of deadly American and Soviet nuclear missiles. People worldwide praised this stunning step toward international peace, and Reagan could be justly proud of his tremendous arms control achievement.

As Reagan's presidency neared its end, many national problems remained. Economists, for example, warned about the mushrooming size of the national debt. Unless the government found a way to repay the billions of dollars it owed, the U.S. economy could collapse.

Above: George and Barbara Bush on his inauguration day
Below: The Reagans and the Bushes descend the Capitol steps together.

Looking back, however, most Americans felt they had experienced an era of good feeling and renewed hope. After eight years of loyal White House service, Vice-President George Bush won the 1988 Republican nomination for president. Bush pointed to the many successes of the Reagan years and promised an even "kinder, gentler" nation. On November 8, 1988, Bush beat his Democratic opponent, Massachusetts governor Michael Dukakis.

"It's been the honor of my life to be your president," seventy-seven-year-old Reagan told Americans in his farewell address. On January 20, 1989, he was pleased to attend the inauguration of George Bush, feeling that the executive office was being passed into capable hands. Soon afterwards he and Nancy journeyed back to California. Wealthy admirers had bought the Reagans a luxury home in the exclusive Bel Air section of Los Angeles.

With the demands of the presidency behind him, Reagan still kept a busy schedule. One task he set for himself was the penning of his presidential memoirs. Occasional speaking tours allowed him to present his views on political issues. Horseback riding, building fences, and other farm activity at Rancho del Cielo still provided the ex-president with hardy exercise.

Whatever Reagan's retirement activities, he will never be forgotten by his fellow Americans. With folksy charm and pure patriotism the actor-turned-politician left his mark upon the nation. In time, history will properly weigh the importance of Ronald Reagan's White House years. But no one will ever question that "The Gipper" ranked among America's most popular presidents.

Above: President and Mrs. Reagan with family members in 1985
Below: Reagan takes a horseback ride on his California ranch.

Above: Nancy joins her husband for his weekly radio address.
Below: The Reagans wave good-bye as they leave presidential days behind.

Chronology of American History

(Shaded area covers events in Ronald Reagan's lifetime.)

About A.D. 982—Eric the Red, born in Norway, reaches Greenland in one of the first European voyages to North America.

About 1000—Leif Ericson (Eric the Red's son) leads what is thought to be the first European expedition to mainland North America; Leif probably lands in Canada.

1492—Christopher Columbus, seeking a sea route from Spain to the Far East, discovers the New World.

1497—John Cabot reaches Canada in the first English voyage to North America.

1513—Ponce de Léon explores Florida in search of the fabled Fountain of Youth.

1519-1521—Hernando Cortés of Spain conquers Mexico.

1534—French explorers led by Jacques Cartier enter the Gulf of St. Lawrence in Canada.

1540—Spanish explorer Francisco Coronado begins exploring the American Southwest, seeking the riches of the mythical Seven Cities of Cibola.

1565—St. Augustine, Florida, the first permanent European town in what is now the United States, is founded by the Spanish.

1607—Jamestown, Virginia, is founded, the first permanent English town in the present-day U.S.

1608—Frenchman Samuel de Champlain founds the village of Quebec, Canada.

1609—Henry Hudson explores the eastern coast of present-day U.S. for the Netherlands; the Dutch then claim parts of New York, New Jersey, Delaware, and Connecticut and name the area New Netherland.

1619—The English colonies' first shipment of black slaves arrives in Jamestown.

1620—English Pilgrims found Massachusetts' first permanent town at Plymouth.

1621—Massachusetts Pilgrims and Indians hold the famous first Thanksgiving feast in colonial America.

1623—Colonization of New Hampshire is begun by the English.

1624—Colonization of present-day New York State is begun by the Dutch at Fort Orange (Albany).

1625—The Dutch start building New Amsterdam (now New York City).

1630—The town of Boston, Massachusetts, is founded by the English Puritans.

1633—Colonization of Connecticut is begun by the English.

1634—Colonization of Maryland is begun by the English.

1636—Harvard, the colonies' first college, is founded in Massachusetts. Rhode Island colonization begins when Englishman Roger Williams founds Providence.

1638—Delaware colonization begins as Swedes build Fort Christina at present-day Wilmington.

1640—Stephen Daye of Cambridge, Massachusetts, prints *The Bay Psalm Book*, the first English-language book published in what is now the U.S.

1643—Swedish settlers begin colonizing Pennsylvania.

About 1650—North Carolina is colonized by Virginia settlers.

1660—New Jersey colonization is begun by the Dutch at present-day Jersey City.

1670—South Carolina colonization is begun by the English near Charleston.

1673—Jacques Marquette and Louis Jolliet explore the upper Mississippi River for France.

1682—Philadelphia, Pennsylvania, is settled. La Salle explores Mississippi River all the way to its mouth in Louisiana and claims the whole Mississippi Valley for France.

1693—College of William and Mary is founded in Williamsburg, Virginia.

1700—Colonial population is about 250,000.

1703—Benjamin Franklin is born in Boston.

1732—George Washington, first president of the U.S., is born in Westmoreland County, Virginia.

1733—James Oglethorpe founds Savannah, Georgia; Georgia is established as the thirteenth colony.

1735—John Adams, second president of the U.S., is born in Braintree, Massachusetts.

1737—William Byrd founds Richmond, Virginia.

1738—British troops are sent to Georgia over border dispute with Spain.

1739—Black insurrection takes place in South Carolina.

1740—English Parliament passes act allowing naturalization of immigrants to American colonies after seven-year residence.

1743—Thomas Jefferson is born in Albemarle County, Virginia. Benjamin Franklin retires at age thirty-seven to devote himself to scientific inquiries and public service.

1744—King George's War begins; France joins war effort against England.

1745—During King George's War, France raids settlements in Maine and New York.

1747—Classes begin at Princeton College in New Jersey.

1748—The Treaty of Aix-la-Chapelle concludes King George's War.

1749—Parliament legally recognizes slavery in colonies and the inauguration of the plantation system in the South. George Washington becomes the surveyor for Culpepper County in Virginia.

1750—Thomas Walker passes through and names Cumberland Gap on his way toward Kentucky region. Colonial population is about 1,200,000.

1751—James Madison, fourth president of the U.S., is born in Port Conway, Virginia. English Parliament passes Currency Act, banning New England colonies from issuing paper money. George Washington travels to Barbados.

1752—Pennsylvania Hospital, the first general hospital in the colonies, is founded in Philadelphia. Benjamin Franklin uses a kite in a thunderstorm to demonstrate that lightning is a form of electricity.

1753—George Washington delivers command that the French withdraw from the Ohio River Valley; French disregard the demand. Colonial population is about 1,328,000.

1754—French and Indian War begins (extends to Europe as the Seven Years' War). Washington surrenders at Fort Necessity.

1755—French and Indians ambush Braddock. Washington becomes commander of Virginia troops.

1756—England declares war on France.

1758—James Monroe, fifth president of the U.S., is born in Westmoreland County, Virginia.

1759—Cherokee Indian war begins in southern colonies; hostilities extend to 1761. George Washington marries Martha Dandridge Custis.

1760—George III becomes king of England. Colonial population is about 1,600,000.

1762—England declares war on Spain.

1763—Treaty of Paris concludes the French and Indian War and the Seven Years' War. England gains Canada and most other French lands east of the Mississippi River.

1764—British pass the Sugar Act to gain tax money from the colonists. The issue of taxation without representation is first introduced in Boston. John Adams marries Abigail Smith.

1765—Stamp Act goes into effect in the colonies. Business virtually stops as almost all colonists refuse to use the stamps.

1766—British repeal the Stamp Act.

1767—John Quincy Adams, sixth president of the U.S. and son of second president John Adams, is born in Braintree, Massachusetts. Andrew Jackson, seventh president of the U.S., is born in Waxhaw settlement, South Carolina.

1769—Daniel Boone sights the Kentucky Territory.

1770—In the Boston Massacre, British soldiers kill five colonists and injure six. Townshend Acts are repealed, thus eliminating all duties on imports to the colonies except tea.

1771—Benjamin Franklin begins his autobiography, a work that he will never complete. The North Carolina assembly passes the "Bloody Act," which makes rioters guilty of treason.

1772—Samuel Adams rouses colonists to consider British threats to self-government.

1773—English Parliament passes the Tea Act. Colonists dressed as Mohawk Indians board British tea ships and toss 342 casks of tea into the water in what becomes known as the Boston Tea Party. William Henry Harrison is born in Charles City County, Virginia.

1774—British close the port of Boston to punish the city for the Boston Tea Party. First Continental Congress convenes in Philadelphia.

1775—American Revolution begins with battles of Lexington and Concord, Massachusetts. Second Continental Congress opens in Philadelphia. George Washington becomes commander-in-chief of the Continental army.

1776—Declaration of Independence is adopted on July 4.

1777—Congress adopts the American flag with thirteen stars and thirteen stripes. John Adams is sent to France to negotiate peace treaty.

1778—France declares war against Great Britain and becomes U.S. ally.

1779—British surrender to Americans at Vincennes. Thomas Jefferson is elected governor of Virginia. James Madison is elected to the Continental Congress.

1780—Benedict Arnold, first American traitor, defects to the British.

1781—Articles of Confederation go into effect. Cornwallis surrenders to George Washington at Yorktown, ending the American Revolution.

1782—American commissioners, including John Adams, sign peace treaty with British in Paris. Thomas Jefferson's wife, Martha, dies. Martin Van Buren is born in Kinderhook, New York.

1784—Zachary Taylor is born near Barboursville, Virginia.

1785—Congress adopts the dollar as the unit of currency. John Adams is made minister to Great Britain. Thomas Jefferson is appointed minister to France.

1786—Shays's Rebellion begins in Massachusetts.

1787—Constitutional Convention assembles in Philadelphia, with George Washington presiding; U.S. Constitution is adopted. Delaware, New Jersey, and Pennsylvania become states.

1788—Virginia, South Carolina, New York, Connecticut, New Hampshire, Maryland, and Massachusetts become states. U.S. Constitution is ratified. New York City is declared U.S. capital.

1789—Presidential electors elect George Washington and John Adams as first president and vice-president. Thomas Jefferson is appointed secretary of state. North Carolina becomes a state. French Revolution begins.

1790—Supreme Court meets for the first time. Rhode Island becomes a state. First national census in the U.S. counts 3,929,214 persons. John Tyler is born in Charles City County, Virginia.

1791—Vermont enters the Union. U.S. Bill of Rights, the first ten amendments to the Constitution, goes into effect. District of Columbia is established. James Buchanan is born in Stony Batter, Pennsylvania.

1792—Thomas Paine publishes *The Rights of Man*. Kentucky becomes a state. Two political parties are formed in the U.S., Federalist and Republican. Washington is elected to a second term, with Adams as vice-president.

1793—War between France and Britain begins; U.S. declares neutrality. Eli Whitney invents the cotton gin; cotton production and slave labor increase in the South.

1794—Eleventh Amendment to the Constitution is passed, limiting federal courts' power. "Whiskey Rebellion" in Pennsylvania protests federal whiskey tax. James Madison marries Dolley Payne Todd.

1795—George Washington signs the Jay Treaty with Great Britain. Treaty of San Lorenzo, between U.S. and Spain, settles Florida boundary and gives U.S. right to navigate the Mississippi. James Polk is born near Pineville, North Carolina.

1796—Tennessee enters the Union. Washington gives his Farewell Address, refusing a third presidential term. John Adams is elected president and Thomas Jefferson vice-president.

1797—Adams recommends defense measures against possible war with France. Napoleon Bonaparte and his army march against Austrians in Italy. U.S. population is about 4,900,000.

1798—Washington is named commander-in-chief of the U.S. Army. Department of the Navy is created. Alien and Sedition Acts are passed. Napoleon's troops invade Egypt and Switzerland.

1799—George Washington dies at Mount Vernon, New York. James Monroe is elected governor of Virginia. French Revolution ends. Napoleon becomes ruler of France.

1800—Thomas Jefferson and Aaron Burr tie for president. U.S. capital is moved from Philadelphia to Washington, D.C. The White House is built as presidents' home. Spain returns Louisiana to France. Millard Fillmore is born in Locke, New York.

1801—After thirty-six ballots, House of Representatives elects Thomas Jefferson president, making Burr vice-president. James Madison is named secretary of state.

1802—Congress abolishes excise taxes. U.S. Military Academy is founded at West Point, New York.

1803—Ohio enters the Union. Louisiana Purchase treaty is signed with France, greatly expanding U.S. territory.

1804—Twelfth Amendment to the Constitution rules that president and vice-president be elected separately. Alexander Hamilton is killed by Vice-President Aaron Burr in a duel. Orleans Territory is established. Napoleon crowns himself emperor of France. Franklin Pierce is born in Hillsborough Lower Village, New Hampshire.

1805—Thomas Jefferson begins his second term as president. Lewis and Clark expedition reaches the Pacific Ocean.

1806—Coinage of silver dollars is stopped; resumes in 1836.

1807—Aaron Burr is acquitted in treason trial. Embargo Act closes U.S. ports to trade.

1808—James Madison is elected president. Congress outlaws importing slaves from Africa. Andrew Johnson is born in Raleigh, North Carolina.

1809—Abraham Lincoln is born near Hodgenville, Kentucky.

1810—U.S. population is 7,240,000.

1811—William Henry Harrison defeats Indians at Tippecanoe. Monroe is named secretary of state.

1812—Louisiana becomes a state. U.S. declares war on Britain (War of 1812). James Madison is reelected president. Napoleon invades Russia.

1813—British forces take Fort Niagara and Buffalo, New York.

1814—Francis Scott Key writes "The Star-Spangled Banner." British troops burn much of Washington, D.C., including the White House. Treaty of Ghent ends War of 1812. James Monroe becomes secretary of war.

1815—Napoleon meets his final defeat at Battle of Waterloo.

1816—James Monroe is elected president. Indiana becomes a state.

1817—Mississippi becomes a state. Construction on Erie Canal begins.

1818—Illinois enters the Union. The present thirteen-stripe flag is adopted. Border between U.S. and Canada is agreed upon.

1819—Alabama becomes a state. U.S. purchases Florida from Spain. Thomas Jefferson establishes the University of Virginia.

1820—James Monroe is reelected. In the Missouri Compromise, Maine enters the Union as a free (non-slave) state.

1821—Missouri enters the Union as a slave state. Santa Fe Trail opens the American Southwest. Mexico declares independence from Spain. Napoleon Bonaparte dies.

1822—U.S. recognizes Mexico and Colombia. Liberia in Africa is founded as a home for freed slaves. Ulysses S. Grant is born in Point Pleasant, Ohio. Rutherford B. Hayes is born in Delaware, Ohio.

1823—Monroe Doctrine closes North and South America to European colonizing or invasion.

1824—House of Representatives elects John Quincy Adams president when none of the four candidates wins a majority in national election. Mexico becomes a republic.

1825—Erie Canal is opened. U.S. population is 11,300,000.

1826—Thomas Jefferson and John Adams both die on July 4, the fiftieth anniversary of the Declaration of Independence.

1828—Andrew Jackson is elected president. Tariff of Abominations is passed, cutting imports.

1829—James Madison attends Virginia's constitutional convention. Slavery is abolished in Mexico. Chester A. Arthur is born in Fairfield, Vermont.

1830—Indian Removal Act to resettle Indians west of the Mississippi is approved.

1831—James Monroe dies in New York City. James A. Garfield is born in Orange, Ohio. Cyrus McCormick develops his reaper.

1832—Andrew Jackson, nominated by the new Democratic Party, is reelected president.

1833—Britain abolishes slavery in its colonies. Benjamin Harrison is born in North Bend, Ohio.

1835—Federal government becomes debt-free for the first time.

1836—Martin Van Buren becomes president. Texas wins independence from Mexico. Arkansas joins the Union. James Madison dies at Montpelier, Virginia.

1837—Michigan enters the Union. U.S. population is 15,900,000. Grover Cleveland is born in Caldwell, New Jersey.

1840—William Henry Harrison is elected president.

1841—President Harrison dies in Washington, D.C., one month after inauguration. Vice-President John Tyler succeeds him.

1843—William McKinley is born in Niles, Ohio.

1844—James Knox Polk is elected president. Samuel Morse sends first telegraphic message.

1845—Texas and Florida become states. Potato famine in Ireland causes massive emigration from Ireland to U.S. Andrew Jackson dies near Nashville, Tennessee.

1846—Iowa enters the Union. War with Mexico begins.

1847—U.S. captures Mexico City.

1848—Zachary Taylor becomes president. Treaty of Guadalupe Hidalgo ends Mexico-U.S. war. Wisconsin becomes a state.

1849—James Polk dies in Nashville, Tennessee.

1850—President Taylor dies in Washington, D.C.; Vice-President Millard Fillmore succeeds him. California enters the Union, breaking tie between slave and free states.

1852—Franklin Pierce is elected president.

1853—Gadsden Purchase transfers Mexican territory to U.S.

1854—"War for Bleeding Kansas" is fought between slave and free states.

1855—Czar Nicholas I of Russia dies, succeeded by Alexander II.

1856—James Buchanan is elected president. In Massacre of Potawatomi Creek, Kansas-slavers are murdered by free-staters. Woodrow Wilson is born in Staunton, Virginia.

1857—William Howard Taft is born in Cincinnati, Ohio.

1858—Minnesota enters the Union. Theodore Roosevelt is born in New York City.

1859—Oregon becomes a state.

1860—Abraham Lincoln is elected president; South Carolina secedes from the Union in protest.

1861—Arkansas, Tennessee, North Carolina, and Virginia secede. Kansas enters the Union as a free state. Civil War begins.

1862—Union forces capture Fort Henry, Roanoke Island, Fort Donelson, Jacksonville, and New Orleans; Union armies are defeated at the battles of Bull Run and Fredericksburg. Martin Van Buren dies in Kinderhook, New York. John Tyler dies near Charles City, Virginia.

1863—Lincoln issues Emancipation Proclamation: all slaves held in rebelling territories are declared free. West Virginia becomes a state.

1864—Abraham Lincoln is reelected. Nevada becomes a state.

1865—Lincoln is assassinated in Washington, D.C., and succeeded by Andrew Johnson. U.S. Civil War ends on May 26. Thirteenth Amendment abolishes slavery. Warren G. Harding is born in Blooming Grove, Ohio.

1867—Nebraska becomes a state. U.S. buys Alaska from Russia for $7,200,000. Reconstruction Acts are passed.

1868—President Johnson is impeached for violating Tenure of Office Act, but is acquitted by Senate. Ulysses S. Grant is elected president. Fourteenth Amendment prohibits voting discrimination. James Buchanan dies in Lancaster, Pennsylvania.

1869—Franklin Pierce dies in Concord, New Hampshire.

1870—Fifteenth Amendment gives blacks the right to vote.

1872—Grant is reelected over Horace Greeley. General Amnesty Act pardons ex-Confederates. Calvin Coolidge is born in Plymouth Notch, Vermont.

1874—Millard Fillmore dies in Buffalo, New York. Herbert Hoover is born in West Branch, Iowa.

1875—Andrew Johnson dies in Carter's Station, Tennessee.

1876—Colorado enters the Union. "Custer's last stand": he and his men are massacred by Sioux Indians at Little Big Horn, Montana.

1877—Rutherford B. Hayes is elected president as all disputed votes are awarded to him.

1880—James A. Garfield is elected president.

1881—President Garfield is assassinated and dies in Elberon, New Jersey. Vice-President Chester A. Arthur succeeds him.

1882—U.S. bans Chinese immigration. Franklin D. Roosevelt is born in Hyde Park, New York.

1884—Grover Cleveland is elected president. Harry S. Truman is born in Lamar, Missouri.

1885—Ulysses S. Grant dies in Mount McGregor, New York.

1886—Statue of Liberty is dedicated. Chester A. Arthur dies in New York City.

1888—Benjamin Harrison is elected president.

1889—North Dakota, South Dakota, Washington, and Montana become states.

1890—Dwight D. Eisenhower is born in Denison, Texas. Idaho and Wyoming become states.

1892—Grover Cleveland is elected president.

1893—Rutherford B. Hayes dies in Fremont, Ohio.

1896—William McKinley is elected president. Utah becomes a state.

1898—U.S. declares war on Spain over Cuba.

1900—McKinley is reelected. Boxer Rebellion against foreigners in China begins.

1901—McKinley is assassinated by anarchist Leon Czolgosz in Buffalo, New York; Theodore Roosevelt becomes president. Benjamin Harrison dies in Indianapolis, Indiana.

1902—U.S. acquires perpetual control over Panama Canal.

1903—Alaskan frontier is settled.

1904—Russian-Japanese War breaks out. Theodore Roosevelt wins presidential election.

1905 — Treaty of Portsmouth signed, ending Russian-Japanese War.

1906 — U.S. troops occupy Cuba.

1907 — President Roosevelt bars all Japanese immigration. Oklahoma enters the Union.

1908 — William Howard Taft becomes president. Grover Cleveland dies in Princeton, New Jersey. Lyndon B. Johnson is born near Stonewall, Texas.

1909 — NAACP is founded under W.E.B. DuBois

1910 — China abolishes slavery.

1911 — Chinese Revolution begins. Ronald Reagan is born in Tampico, Illinois.

1912 — Woodrow Wilson is elected president. Arizona and New Mexico become states.

1913 — Federal income tax is introduced in U.S. through the Sixteenth Amendment. Richard Nixon is born in Yorba Linda, California. Gerald Ford is born in Omaha, Nebraska.

1914 — World War I begins.

1915 — British liner *Lusitania* is sunk by German submarine.

1916 — Wilson is reelected president.

1917 — U.S. breaks diplomatic relations with Germany. Czar Nicholas of Russia abdicates as revolution begins. U.S. declares war on Austria-Hungary. John F. Kennedy is born in Brookline, Massachusetts.

1918 — Wilson proclaims "Fourteen Points" as war aims. On November 11, armistice is signed between Allies and Germany.

1919 — Eighteenth Amendment prohibits sale and manufacture of intoxicating liquors. Wilson presides over first League of Nations; wins Nobel Peace Prize. Theodore Roosevelt dies in Oyster Bay, New York.

1920 — Nineteenth Amendment (women's suffrage) is passed. Warren Harding is elected president.

1921 — Adolf Hitler's stormtroopers begin to terrorize political opponents.

1922 — Irish Free State is established. Soviet states form USSR. Benito Mussolini forms Fascist government in Italy.

1923 — President Harding dies in San Francisco, California; he is succeeded by Vice-President Calvin Coolidge.

1924 — Coolidge is elected president. Woodrow Wilson dies in Washington, D.C. James Carter is born in Plains, Georgia. George Bush is born in Milton, Massachusetts.

1925 — Hitler reorganizes Nazi Party and publishes first volume of *Mein Kampf.*

1926 — Fascist youth organizations founded in Germany and Italy. Republic of Lebanon proclaimed.

1927 — Stalin becomes Soviet dictator. Economic conference in Geneva attended by fifty-two nations.

1928 — Herbert Hoover is elected president. U.S. and many other nations sign Kellogg-Briand pacts to outlaw war.

1929 — Stock prices in New York crash on "Black Thursday"; the Great Depression begins.

1930 — Bank of U.S. and its many branches close (most significant bank failure of the year). William Howard Taft dies in Washington, D.C.

1931 — Emigration from U.S. exceeds immigration for first time as Depression deepens.

1932 — Franklin D. Roosevelt wins presidential election in a Democratic landslide.

1933 — First concentration camps are erected in Germany. U.S. recognizes USSR and resumes trade. Twenty-First Amendment repeals prohibition. Calvin Coolidge dies in Northampton, Massachusetts.

1934 — Severe dust storms hit Plains states. President Roosevelt passes U.S. Social Security Act.

1936 — Roosevelt is reelected. Spanish Civil War begins. Hitler and Mussolini form Rome-Berlin Axis.

1937 — Roosevelt signs Neutrality Act.

1938 — Roosevelt sends appeal to Hitler and Mussolini to settle European problems amicably.

1939 — Germany takes over Czechoslovakia and invades Poland, starting World War II.

1940—Roosevelt is reelected for a third term.

1941—Japan bombs Pearl Harbor, U.S. declares war on Japan. Germany and Italy declare war on U.S.; U.S. then declares war on them.

1942—Allies agree not to make separate peace treaties with the enemies. U.S. government transfers more than 100,000 Nisei (Japanese-Americans) from west coast to inland concentration camps.

1943—Allied bombings of Germany begin.

1944—Roosevelt is reelected for a fourth term. Allied forces invade Normandy on D-Day.

1945—President Franklin D. Roosevelt dies in Warm Springs, Georgia; Vice-President Harry S. Truman succeeds him. Mussolini is killed; Hitler commits suicide. Germany surrenders. U.S. drops atomic bomb on Hiroshima; Japan surrenders; end of World War II.

1946—U.N. General Assembly holds its first session in London. Peace conference of twenty-one nations is held in Paris.

1947—Peace treaties are signed in Paris. "Cold War" is in full swing.

1948—U.S. passes Marshall Plan Act, providing $17 billion in aid for Europe. U.S. recognizes new nation of Israel. India and Pakistan become free of British rule. Truman is elected president.

1949—Republic of Eire is proclaimed in Dublin. Russia blocks land route access from Western Germany to Berlin; airlift begins. U.S., France, and Britain agree to merge their zones of occupation in West Germany. Apartheid program begins in South Africa.

1950—Riots in Johannesburg, South Africa, against apartheid. North Korea invades South Korea. U.N. forces land in South Korea and recapture Seoul.

1951—Twenty-Second Amendment limits president to two terms.

1952—Dwight D. Eisenhower resigns as supreme commander in Europe and is elected president.

1953—Stalin dies; struggle for power in Russia follows. Rosenbergs are executed for espionage.

1954—U.S. and Japan sign mutual defense agreement.

1955—Blacks in Montgomery, Alabama, boycott segregated bus lines.

1956—Eisenhower is reelected president. Soviet troops march into Hungary.

1957—U.S. agrees to withdraw ground forces from Japan. Russia launches first satellite, *Sputnik.*

1958—European Common Market comes into being. Alaska becomes the forty-ninth state. Fidel Castro begins war against Batista government in Cuba.

1959—Hawaii becomes fiftieth state. Castro becomes premier of Cuba. De Gaulle is proclaimed president of the Fifth Republic of France.

1960—Historic debates between Senator John F. Kennedy and Vice-President Richard Nixon are televised. Kennedy is elected president. Brezhnev becomes president of USSR.

1961—Berlin Wall is constructed. Kennedy and Khrushchev confer in Vienna. In Bay of Pigs incident, Cubans trained by CIA attempt to overthrow Castro.

1962—U.S. military council is established in South Vietnam.

1963—Riots and beatings by police and whites mark civil rights demonstrations in Birmingham, Alabama; 30,000 troops are called out, Martin Luther King, Jr., is arrested. Freedom marchers descend on Washington, D.C., to demonstrate. President Kennedy is assassinated in Dallas, Texas; Vice-President Lyndon B. Johnson is sworn in as president.

1964—U.S. aircraft bomb North Vietnam. Johnson is elected president. Herbert Hoover dies in New York City.

1965—U.S. combat troops arrive in South Vietnam.

1966—Thousands protest U.S. policy in Vietnam. National Guard quells race riots in Chicago.

1967—Six-Day War between Israel and Arab nations.

1968—Martin Luther King, Jr., is assassinated in Memphis, Tennessee. Senator Robert Kennedy is assassinated in Los Angeles. Riots and police brutality take place at Democratic National Convention in Chicago. Richard Nixon is elected president. Czechoslovakia is invaded by Soviet troops.

1969—Dwight D. Eisenhower dies in Washington, D.C. Hundreds of thousands of people in several U.S. cities demonstrate against Vietnam War.

1970—Four Vietnam War protesters are killed by National Guardsmen at Kent State University in Ohio.

1971—Twenty-Sixth Amendment allows eighteen-year-olds to vote.

1972—Nixon visits Communist China; is reelected president in near-record landslide. Watergate affair begins when five men are arrested in the Watergate hotel complex in Washington, D.C. Nixon announces resignations of aides Haldeman, Ehrlichman, and Dean and Attorney General Kleindienst as a result of Watergate-related charges. Harry S. Truman dies in Kansas City, Missouri.

1973—Vice-President Spiro Agnew resigns; Gerald Ford is named vice-president. Vietnam peace treaty is formally approved after nineteen months of negotiations. Lyndon B. Johnson dies in San Antonio, Texas.

1974—As a result of Watergate cover-up, impeachment is considered; Nixon resigns and Ford becomes president. Ford pardons Nixon and grants limited amnesty to Vietnam War draft evaders and military deserters.

1975—U.S. civilians are evacuated from Saigon, South Vietnam, as Communist forces complete takeover of South Vietnam.

1976—U.S. celebrates its Bicentennial. James Earl Carter becomes president.

1977—Carter pardons most Vietnam draft evaders, numbering some 10,000.

1980—Ronald Reagan is elected president.

1981—President Reagan is shot in the chest in assassination attempt. Sandra Day O'Connor is appointed first woman justice of the Supreme Court.

1983—U.S. troops invade island of Grenada.

1984—Reagan is reelected president. Democratic candidate Walter Mondale's running mate, Geraldine Ferraro, is the first woman selected for vice-president by a major U.S. political party.

1985—Soviet Communist Party secretary Konstantin Chernenko dies; Mikhail Gorbachev succeeds him. U.S. and Soviet officials discuss arms control in Geneva. Reagan and Gorbachev hold summit conference in Geneva. Racial tensions accelerate in South Africa.

1986—Space shuttle *Challenger* explodes shortly after takeoff; crew of seven dies. U.S. bombs bases in Libya. Corazon Aquino defeats Ferdinand Marcos in Philippine presidential election.

1987—Iraqi missile rips the U.S. frigate *Stark* in the Persian Gulf, killing thirty-seven American sailors. Congress holds hearings to investigate sale of U.S. arms to Iran to finance Nicaraguan *contra* movement.

1988—George Bush is elected president. President Reagan and Soviet leader Gorbachev sign INF treaty, eliminating intermediate nuclear forces. Severe drought sweeps the United States.

1989—East Germany opens Berlin Wall, allowing citizens free exit. Communists lose control of governments in Poland, Romania, and Czechoslovakia. Chinese troops massacre over 1,000 pro-democracy student demonstrators in Beijing's Tiananmen Square.

1990—Iraq annexes Kuwait, provoking the threat of war. East and West Germany are reunited. The Cold War between the United States and the Soviet Union comes to a close. Several Soviet republics make moves toward independence.

1991—Backed by a coalition of members of the United Nations, U.S. troops drive Iraqis from Kuwait. Latvia, Lithuania, and Estonia withdraw from the USSR. The Soviet Union dissolves as its republics secede to form a commonwealth of free nations.

1992—U.N. forces fail to stop fighting in territories of former Yugoslavia. More than fifty people are killed and more than six hundred buildings burned in rioting in Los Angeles. U.S. unemployment reaches eight-year high. Hurricane Andrew devastates southern Florida and parts of Louisiana. International relief supplies and troops are sent to combat famine and violence in Somalia.

1993—U.S.-led forces use airplanes and missiles to attack military targets in Iraq. William Jefferson Clinton becomes the forty-second U.S. president.

Index

Page numbers in boldface type indicate illustrations.

About the Author

Zachary Kent grew up in Little Falls, New Jersey, and received an English degree from St. Lawrence University. Following college he worked at a New York City literary agency for two years and then launched his writing career. To support himself while writing, he has worked as a taxi driver, a shipping clerk, and a house painter. Mr. Kent has had a lifelong interest in American history. Studying the U.S. presidents was his childhood hobby. His collection of presidential items includes books, pictures, and games, as well as several autographed letters.